Parties Kids Love

by Mike Artell & Pam Schiller

Illustrated by Mike Artell

GoodYearBooks

An Imprint of ScottForesman
A Division of HarperCollinsPublishers

GoodYearBooks

are available for most basic curriculum subjects
plus many enrichment areas. For more GoodYearBooks,
contact your local bookseller or educational dealer.
For a complete catalog with information about
other GoodYearBooks, please write:

GoodYearBooks

ScottForesman
1900 East Lake Avenue
Glenview, IL 60025

Design by Christine Ronan.

ISBN 0-673-36229-9

1 2 3 4 5 6 7 8 9 - DP - 04 03 02 01 00 99 98 97 96

CONTENTS

Introduction

*I*t's party time! Every child's dream—every adult's nightmare. If you find yourself panicking at the thought of planning and executing a party for three-, four-, five-, or six-year-olds, relax. This book is designed to help you with every aspect of party planning from creating a unique theme and invitations to decorations, entertainment, and even a creative menu.

We've also included a section called "Preschool Pointers," a collection of hints for successfully managing a group of small children. All you have to do is follow the simple directions in this book. Then sit back and take all the credit for a fantastic and memorable party.

4

How to Use This Book

There are three categories of parties described in this book: Birthday, Holiday, and Just for Fun. Each category includes directions and suggestions for four different parties.

Each party guide is built around a special Feature and includes an invitation (Fanfare), a list of possible activities for entertainment (Fun), a menu (Food), a list of suggested prizes (Favors), some art for decorations (Frills), information about the theme (Facts), and several stories to read together (Fiction).

Feel free to pick and choose what you want for a specific party, to mix and match from several parties, or to add your own creative and unique ideas. The most important thing is that everyone have FUN. Even you!

So let's have a party!

Preschool Pointers

Guests

A good rule of thumb is to plan for one guest for each year of the honoree's age, and then add two. Young children have a difficult time dividing their attention among several friends and can become overwhelmed and frustrated by attempting to accommodate too many people.

Activities

❀ Children participate more productively when they have choices. The honoree might help choose the theme and activities for the party, and the guests will be much more cooperative if they are allowed some choices during the party. Remember, though, too many choices are confusing.

❀ Children have very short attention spans. Balance active games with passive activities. Most young children have a difficult time sitting still for longer than 10 to 15 minutes.

❀ Whenever possible, let the children do things for themselves. For example, you might let the children pour their own juice, make their own art sculptures, or design their own hats.

❀ Activity and curiosity are natural characteristics of all young children. Parties are no exception, so be prepared, and go with, not against, the flow.

❀ Put decorations down at the eye level of the children. Keep decorations to a minimum. Too much decorating is overstimulating, and the normal activity of the group will escalate.

Helpers

Always have other adults present at the party. You'll need the extra hands. Invite friends, relatives, or parents of one of the guests.

Timing

❀ The best length of time for the party is 1 1/2 hours. If the party is too long, the children will lose interest.

❀ Be sure to include the starting and ending time of the party on the invitation, so you're not trapped into providing hours of free babysitting services.

BIRTHDAY PARTIES

A WHALE of a Party

Here's how to make a "whale" of an invitation: Buy a small bag of oval-shaped balloons and inflate a balloon. Pinch the opening (the part you blow into) closed with your fingers, but don't tie a knot in the balloon. Next, draw two eyes and a big whale mouth on the other end of the balloon with a permanent marker or paint pen. Let it dry for just a moment.

Release the air from the balloon. Then slip the opening through the hole in the paper tail containing the invitation information. Mail your "balloon whale" invitations to the guests.

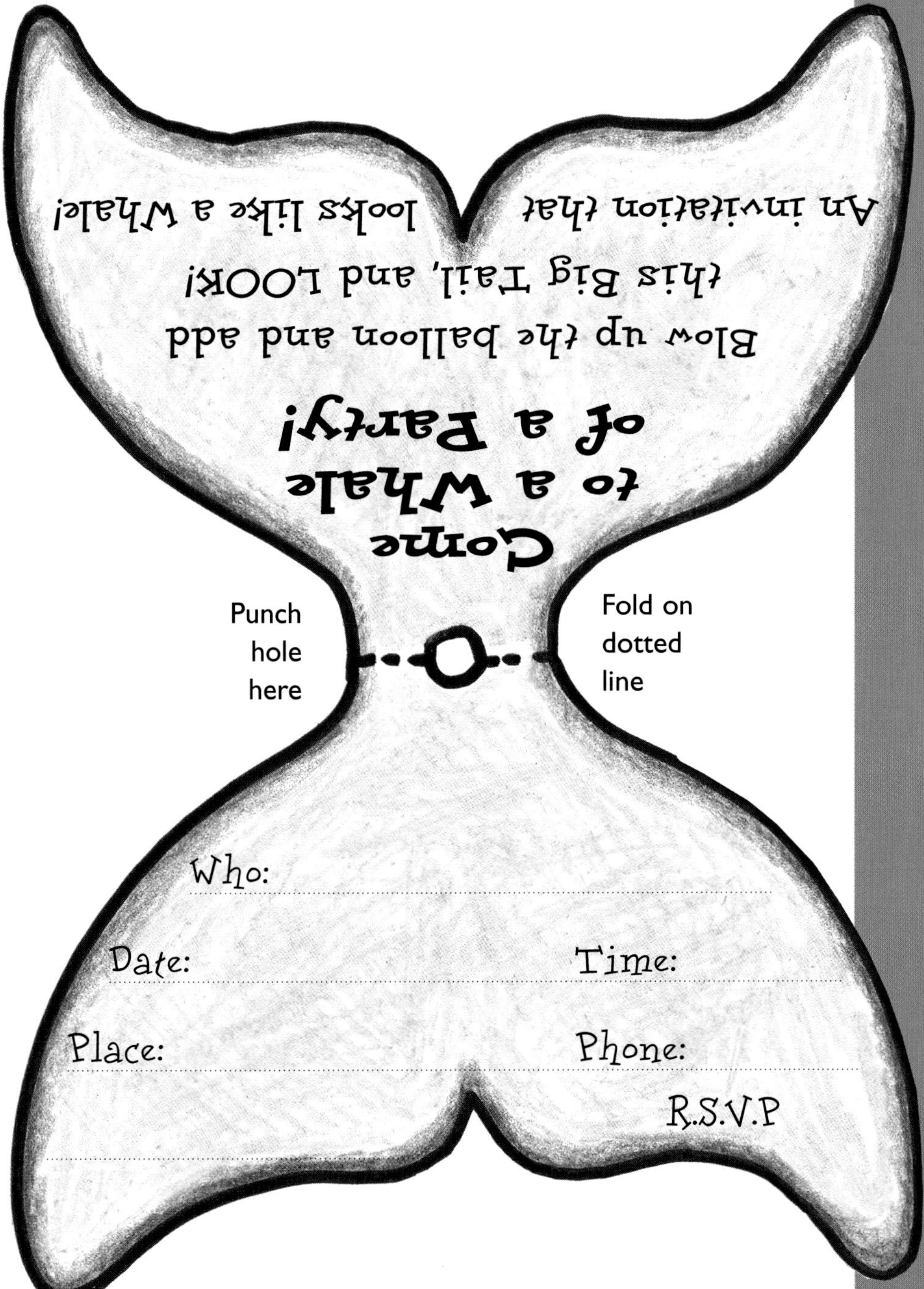

An invitation that looks like a Whale!

Blow up the balloon and add this Big Tail, and LOOK!

Come to a Whale of a Party!

Punch hole here

Fold on dotted line

Who:
....

Date: ....

Time: ....

Place: ....

Phone: ....

R.S.V.P

....

Fan-Fare

or

how to

invite

everybody

to the party!

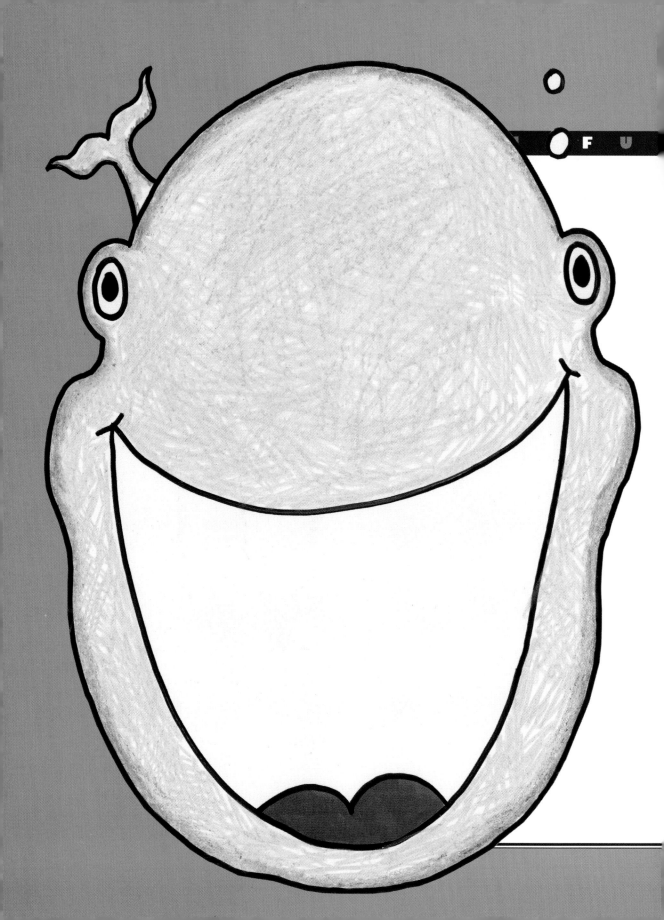

A Whale of a Party

Feed the Whale

Copy and glue the whale on page 12 to the bottom of a cardboard box. Cut a hole in the whale's mouth, and encourage the children to throw a beanbag in the whale's mouth.

Pin the Tail on the Whale

Copy and place the illustration on page 19 on the refrigerator or on another metallic surface (try a cookie sheet). Make copies of the tail below and cut them out. Glue a magnet on the back of each. Blindfold the children, and let them try to put the tail on the whale.

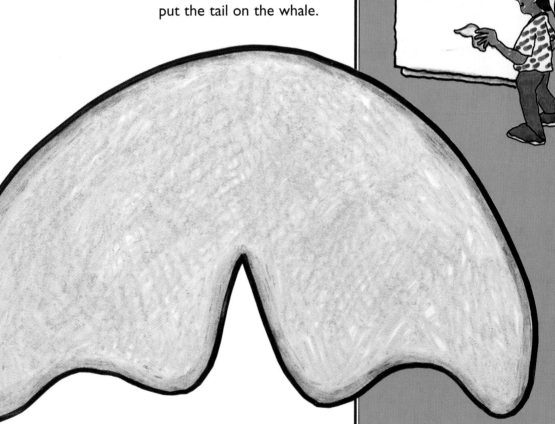

More Fun

Baby Whale Pick-Up

Stage a relay race. Divide the children into two teams. Place an equal number of goldfish-shaped crackers in two shallow containers and place them 15 to 20 feet from the teams. Place an empty container with each team. Give each team a spoon. Instruct the children to run one at a time to the container of goldfish, pick up a goldfish with the spoon, return to their group, drop the goldfish into the empty container, and hand the spoon to the next runner. Continue until one team transfers all the goldfish between its containers.

Jump the Seaweed

Wrap some seaweed (or some shredded crêpe paper) around a jump rope. Let the children take turns jumping the rope. See who can perform the most jumps. (Very small children can't do overhead jumping, but they do a great job jumping over a rope swung back and forth low to the ground.)

Bubble Bump

Have the children pair off. Give each pair a clear balloon which they are to keep off the ground by holding it between their tummies (see illustration). The object is for the pair to maneuver together through an "iceberg" obstacle course to a cardboard box and then to deposit the balloon in the box. The "icebergs" are pieces of foam laid on the floor. If the balloon falls, the children may pick it up with their hands, but while maneuvering, they must keep the balloon suspended with "tummy power" only.

A Whale of a Tale

Gather the children in a circle and have them perform the actions as they repeat after you.

Adult says: Gather 'round all you little minnows, 'cause I'm going to tell you a whale of a tale. Now, repeat after me:

Down in the sea,
(Down in the sea,)

In the salty ol' sea,
(In the salty ol' sea,)

A whale wiggled wildly
(A whale wiggled wildly)
(Everybody wiggles.)

In the warm, wet water.
(In the warm, wet water.)

He saw seven shrimp
(He saw seven shrimp)
(Everybody makes "big" eyes and looks around.)

Swimming slowly in the sea.
(Swimming slowly in the sea.) *(Everybody makes "swimming" motions.)*

Whales wiggle wildly, shrimp swim slowly,
(Whales wiggle wildly, shrimp swim slowly,)

(Repeat above actions.)

There's a lot going on in the salty ol' sea. (There's a lot going on in the salty ol' sea.)

Down in the sea,
(Down in the sea,)

In the salty ol' sea,
(In the salty ol' sea,)

A whale wiggled wildly in the warm wet water.
(A whale wiggled wildly in the warm wet water.)

(Repeat actions above.)

Down in the sea,
(Down in the sea,)

In the salty ol' sea,
(In the salty ol' sea,)

Someone saw seven shrimp swim slowly.
(Someone saw seven shrimp swim slowly.)

(Repeat actions above.)

There's a lot going on in the salty ol' sea.
(There's a lot going on in the salty ol' sea.)

Food

Tuna Boats

Cut tuna sandwiches diagonally into quarter sections. Slice an apple into $1/4$" thick, round slices. Place a tuna sandwich quarter on top of each apple slice, like a sail (see illustration).

Goldfish Crackers

Purchase goldfish-shaped crackers from your local grocery store.

Whale Spout Cupcakes

Bake and ice cupcakes. Purchase licorice or cherry candy "laces," and cut them into 4" lengths. Have the children decorate their own cupcakes by poking the candy laces into the center of the cupcakes to make a whale spout (see illustration).

Goldfish

Tuna Boats

Whale Spout Cupcakes

16

Sea
Foam
Floats

Ocean
Blue Ice
Cream

Ocean Blue Ice Cream

Allow a gallon of vanilla ice cream to soften. Stir in 2 teaspoons of blue cake icing coloring or 2 tablespoons of blue food coloring. Refreeze the ice cream.

Sea Foam Floats

Put a scoop of Ocean Blue ice cream into a clear plastic glass. Add two or three drops of green food coloring to your favorite lemon-lime beverage. Pour over the ice cream. Serve with long blue straws and blue or green plastic spoons.

Favors and Frills

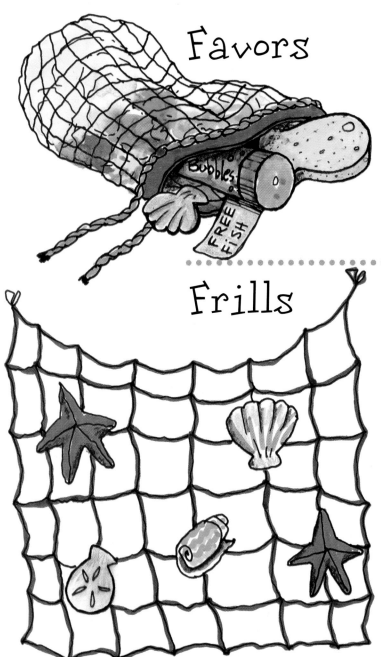

Favors

Inside bags of netted material, each tied with a piece of small rope, place some **sea shells**, a few **sponge fish** for th tub, a **coupon** for free **goldfish** from a local pe store, and a container of **bubbles** with a bubble wand.

Frills

Hang **fishnet** on the walls.

Place **seashells** around the room.

Wear a **sailor's hat**.

Drape **blue crêpe paper** from the ceiling with clear, bubble-like balloons all around.

Draw **whale outlines** on butcher paper, and tape them near the front door. When guests arrive, have each of them write his or he name on one of the whales.

Fact

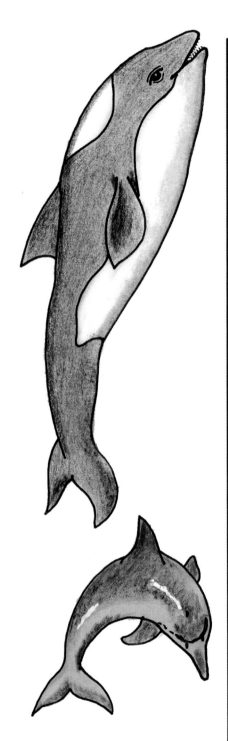

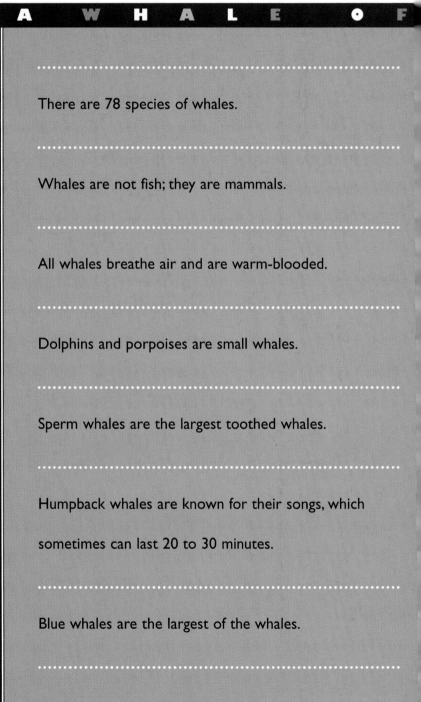

There are 78 species of whales.

Whales are not fish; they are mammals.

All whales breathe air and are warm-blooded.

Dolphins and porpoises are small whales.

Sperm whales are the largest toothed whales.

Humpback whales are known for their songs, which

sometimes can last 20 to 30 minutes.

Blue whales are the largest of the whales.

Fiction

Davis, M. S. A. *Garden of Whales.* Camden House, 1993.

A child imagines living the life of a whale.

Sheldon, Dyan. *The Whale's Song.* Dial, 1991. Lily's

grandmother tells a story of how, when she was a little

girl, she waited by the ocean for the whales to come.

Wells, R. E. *Is a Blue Whale the Biggest Thing There Is?*

Albert Whitman, 1993. This book compares the size of

things like mountains, other planets, and Earth to the

blue whale.

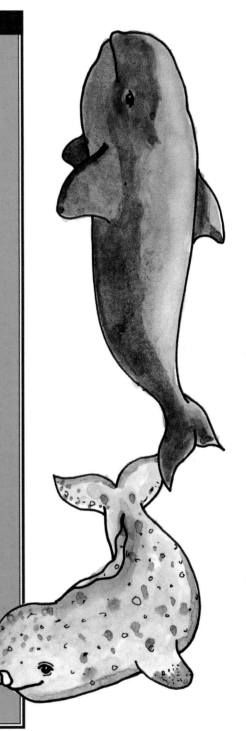

TEDDY BEAR
Picnic

Come to my Teddy Bear Party!

Name: ....

Place: ....

....

Date: .... Time: ....

Phone: ....

Bring your Favorite Bear!

By mail, send each guest a 9" by 12" white catalog envelope (available at office supply stores) covered with multicolored stamp imprints of teddy bears. You can find stamps at discount stores, teacher supply stores, some gift shops, or office supply stores. Inside is a handmade, construction-paper teddy bear holding an invitation. The invitation tells the guest to bring his or her own teddy bear to the party.

Teddy Bear Picnic

F U N

BRITTANYS

BEAR

Make a Flag

Provide construction
paper, scissors, and glue.
Encourage the children
to design a flag for the
Teddy Bear Parade. Use
small dowels or extra
long straws as flagpoles.

Bear Kites

Give each child a 12" by 18" piece of brown construction paper and a bear pattern cut from posterboard. Use this bear to create a pattern. Let the children decorate their bears with scraps of fabric, wallpaper, sequins, buttons, and ribbon. Punch a hole in each bear, and tie on a 2' piece of yarn. Have the children run with their kites; the bears will follow.

More Fun

Teddy Bear Relay Race

Ask the children to get their teddy bears. Be sure to have extra bears on hand for anyone who forgets to bring one. Divide the children into two teams and stand them in separate lines. Place one laundry basket or box approximately 25 feet in front of each line. Have the children run, one at a time, from their starting line to their basket, drop their bear in, and run back to tag the next person in line, who then repeats the pattern. The first team that gets all the bears in the basket and their last runner back to the starting line wins. Treat everyone to a snack of gummy bears.

Teddy Bear Parade

Play marching music and let the children parade around the yard, carrying their bears and waving their flags.

Food

Goodnight Bear Sandwiches

For each child, spread a slice of bread with margarine. Let the children use a cookie cutter to cut a bear shape from a slice of cheese. Have them lay their cheese bears on the bread slices. Then give them half a slice of bread to lay over the bottom half of their bears. Toast the sandwiches, and serve.

Stick Snacks

Cut carrots and celery into 3" sticks.

Teddy Grahams®

Serve bear-shaped graham crackers, available from your supermarket.

28

Honey Nut Cheerios®

Little bears love honey. Give each little bear a small cup of dry Honey Nut Cheerios®.

Bear Paw Apple Turnovers

Prepare pie dough ahead of time. Provide each child with a 6" circle of the dough. Have the children put 2 tablespoons of apple pie filling in the middle of their dough circle. Show them how to fold the circle in half and pinch the edges together. Cut three lines in each turnover to make it look more like a "paw." Bake at 375° for 12 minutes. Let them cool before you serve them.

Favors and Frills

Favors

Parade flags used in the Fun section

Small gift jars or plastic squeeze bottles of **honey**

Small bags of **gummy bears**

Baby teddy bear **masks**

Wooden teddy bear silhouette **stamps**, used in making the invitations

Frills

Decorate the room and yard with **kites**, **streamers**, and **pinwheels**.

Make your own **pinwheels** for decoration. Copy or trace the pattern onto colored construction paper, leftover wallpaper, or wrapping paper. Cut out the pattern, and then pull all the ends to the center. Put a thumbtack or pin through the center and into a small dowel rod. Note: If children will be playing with these, make sure your fastener is secure.

Spread red and white checked **paper tablecloths** on the ground for picnickers.

Make individual **picnic baskets** to hold each child's food. Weave strips of brown paper sacks or construction paper. Cover shoe boxes with your weavings.

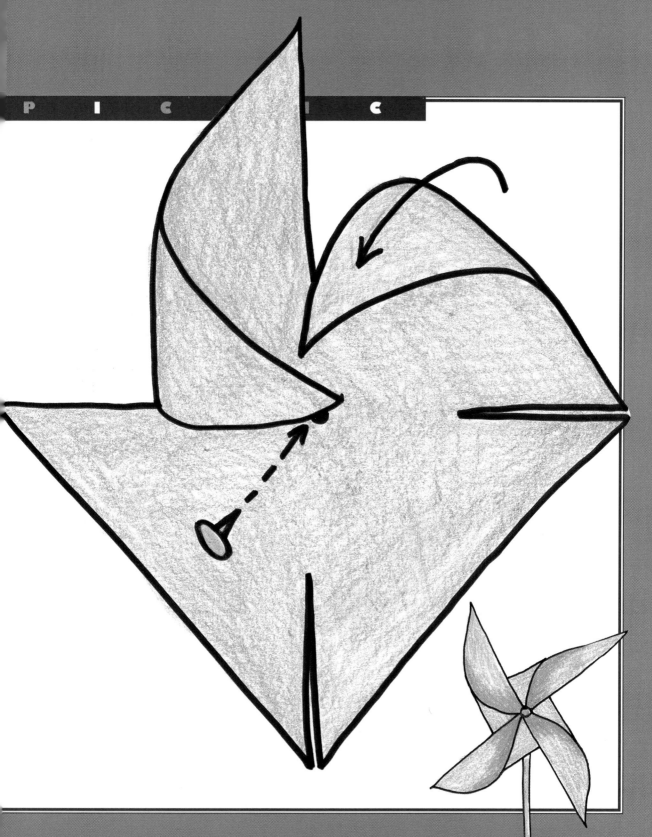

Facts

TEDDY BEAR

Teddy bears are the most popular children's toy.

There are seven species of bears.

Some animals that look like bears, such as pandas and koalas, are not bears.

The first teddy bear was made and named for President Teddy Roosevelt because he refused to shoot a black bear while on a hunting trip.

There are many famous make-believe bears, such as Smokey, Yogi, and the Berenstains.

The group of stars commonly called the Big Dipper is one of the most recognized constellations. Its official name is Ursa Major, "The Great Bear."

Fiction

Brett, Jan. *Goldilocks and the Three Bears.* Putnam, 1987. This traditional tale is beautifully illustrated.

....

Kennedy, Jimmy. *The Teddy Bears' Picnic.* Simon & Schuster, 1991. Teddy bears have their picnic in the woods on a special day.

....

Martin, Bill, Jr. *Brown Bear, Brown Bear, What Do You See?* Holt, 1983. A big book of animals and colors, with each animal asking the next, "What do you see?"

....

Newman, Nanette. *There's a Bear in the Bath!* Harcourt, 1994. Jan the bear drinks coffee, works crossword puzzles, and dances the tango. He also likes to relax in the tub.

....

Rosen, Michael. *We're Going on a Bear Hunt.* Macmillan, 1989. A father, four children, and a dog set out on a bear hunt.

MAD HATTER *Party*

Featuring:

Hats!

Hats!

Hats!

You're invited to a

MAD HATTER *Party*

When:

Time:

Where:

Given by:

Phone no.:

Wear a Funny Hat!!

Fan-Fare

Hat-vitation

Photocopy the two hats and color the front of the hat. Cut out both hat pieces and glue them back-to-back. For a sturdier invitation, "sandwich" a piece of construction paper between the two hat cutouts and glue all three pieces together. Place invitations into envelopes and mail to each guest.

Mad Hatter Party

MAD HATTER

Make a Crazy Hat

Paper plates make a good base from which the children can create hats. Cut the center out of the plates and let the children decorate the rim. Provide them with construction paper, yarn, tissue paper, old costume jewelry, ribbon, and other scrap materials to decorate their hats.

Crazy Hat Style Show

Encourage the children to model their hats and describe them to their friends.

Mad Hatter Says

Play this game as you would play "Simon Says"; simply substitute "Mad Hatter" for "Simon."

Musical Hats

Have the children form a circle. Place several hats, one less than children, in the center of the circle. Encourage children to march around the circle to music. When you stop the music, the children grab the hats. The child without a hat leaves the circle. Remove one or two hats, and continue the game until only one child has a hat.

Drop the Penny in the Hat

Let the children see how many pennies they can drop into a hat.

Hat Song

Sing "The Hat Song" to the tune of "She'll Be Comin' 'round the Mountain." Have the children sit in a circle and perform the actions as they sing.

Put your hat on your head, clap your hands.
(Clap twice.)
Put your hat on your head, clap your hands.
(Clap twice.)
Put your hat on your head, put your hat on your head,
Put your hat on your head, clap your hands.
(Clap twice.)

Boys and girls change hats, clap your hands. (Clap twice.)
Boys and girls change hats, clap your hands. (Clap twice.)
Boys and girls change hats, boys and girls change hats,
Boys and girls change hats, clap your hands. (Clap twice.)

Get your hat from your neighbor, clap your hands.
(Clap twice.)
Get your hat from your neighbor, clap your hands.
(Clap twice.)
Get your hat from your neighbor, get your hat from your neighbor,
Get your hat from your neighbor, clap your hands.
(Clap twice.)

Put your hat on your head, put your hat on your head,
Put your hat on your head, clap your hands.
(Clap twice.)

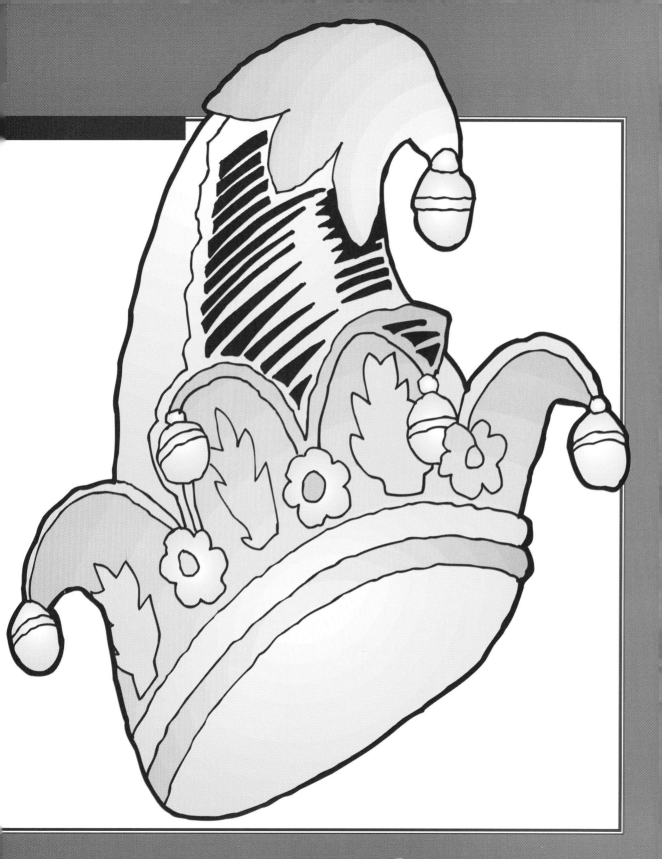

Food

Mad Hatter Hash

In a bowl, combine the following ingredients:

$1/2$ cup of chocolate chips

1 cup of raisins

1 cup of miniature marshmallows

1 cup of peanuts

1 cup of coconut

Serve on small plates or in bowls

Peppermint Pats

In a mixing bowl, combine 4 cups of sifted confectioner's sugar, $2/3$ cup of sweetened condensed milk, a few drops of green food coloring, and $1/4$ teaspoon of peppermint extract. Spoon onto wax paper, and press with fork tines. Makes about 30 patties.

Mad Hatter Hash

Peppermint Pats

Tutti-Frutti Ice Sparkle

Mad Hatter Tea Cake Creations

Tutti-Frutti Ice Sparkle

Mix one package of lime drink powder with $2/3$ cup of sugar and 4 cups of water. Pour the mixture into ice trays. Do the same with one package each of orange and cherry drink powder. In tall, clear glasses, put one ice cube of each flavor. Then fill with chilled carbonated lemon-lime drink. Add half a slice of orange and serve. This looks great with a red-and-white striped straw.

Mad Hatter Tea Cake Creations

Give each child a sponge-cake dessert cup (the kind grocery stores sell for strawberry shortcakes). Provide berries, slices of fruit, shredded coconut, and whipped cream. Encourage the children to treat their dessert cups like hats and decorate them with the goodies.

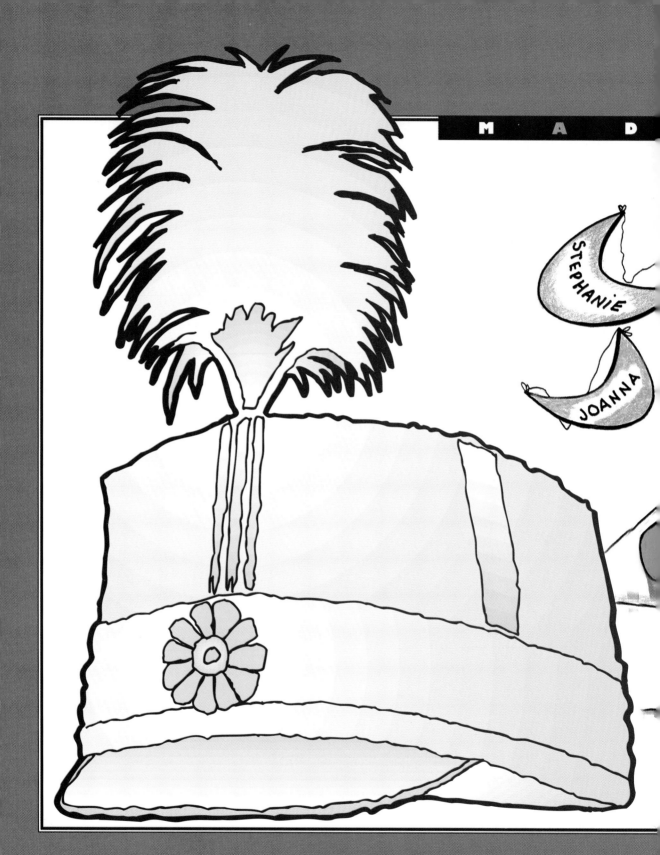

HATTER PARTY

Favors

Frills

Crazy Hats from the Fun section

Inexpensive plastic sun visors with each child's name written on them with a paint pen.

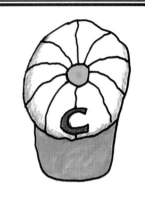

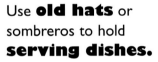

Use **old hats** or sombreros to hold **serving dishes.** Also useful are football and motorcycle helmets, baby bonnets, and sock caps.

Hang real or paper cutout **hats** and **caps** as **decorations.**

Photocopy the drawings of the **hats** on pages 39 and 42 for each child. Have each color a hat drawing and put his or her name at the bottom. Use these drawings as **placemats.**

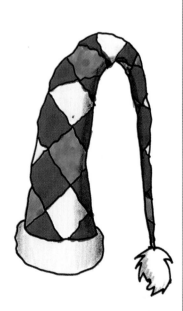

Facts

M A D   H A T T E R

People wear hats for lots of reasons, including protection and decoration.

Hats can tell a lot about the people who wear them. Some hats tell you about people's jobs (coal miner's hat, firefighter's hat, police officer's hat, etc.). In some cultures, a person's hat shows things such as whether the person is married.

The size of hat you wear is determined by the circumference of your head. Use a tape measure to see what size hat each child wears.

Fiction

Howard, Elizabeth. *Aunt Flossie's Hats*. Clarion, 1991. As Aunt Flossie shows her hat collection to her nieces, she tells a story of a time she wore each hat.

....

Keats, Ezra Jack. *Jennie's Hat*. Harper, 1966. When Jennie's beautiful, handmade hat is destroyed, birds help her make a new one.

....

Nister, Ernest. *Special Days*. Philomel, 1989. This miniature pull-tab book follows young children as they build castles, play on a tree swing, enjoy tea parties, and share special days.

....

Pienkowski, Jan. *Little Monsters: Eggs for Tea*. Doubleday, 1990. Five little monsters share eggs cooked in different ways—poached, fried, scrambled, and boiled.

WESTERN ROUNDUP

Ya'll Come On Down!

for a WESTERN ROUNDUP PARTY!

This party is
being given by

Date:

Time:

Where:

Phone:

Dress in your Favorite
COUNTRY & WESTERN
CLOTHING!

Photocopy the two boots and color the front of the boot. Cut out both boot pieces and glue them back-to-back. For a sturdier invitation, "sandwich" a piece of construction paper between the two boot cutouts and glue all three pieces together. Your local "quick print" shop will probably also have heavier weight sheets of colored paper onto which you can photocopy the boot drawings if you want to eliminate the coloring step. Place invitations into envelopes and mail to each guest.

Western Roundup

Horseshoes

Use commercial horseshoes or make your own set. To make it yourself, you'll need two $3/4$" dowels (10" long), two 10" squares of 1" Styrofoam, and eight rubber rings from canning jars.

Stick Horse Relays

Use commercial stick horses, or make them yourself. For each one, you'll need a $3/4$" dowel (28" long), a sock, buttons, felt, and yarn. Stuff the sock with crumpled paper or scrap material. Add button eyes, felt ears, and a yarn mane. Attach the head to the dowel with a rubber band. Divide the children into two teams, and let them compete in a relay race as they "ride" their horses.

Covered Wagon Golf

Make covered wagon tunnels using 9" by 12" sheets of brown construction paper. Curve the sheets into tunnel shapes and tape them to the floor in a pattern similar to croquet hoops. Give children tennis balls and clubs made from empty wrapping paper tubes. Play the game as you would play croquet. Children will enjoy simply trying to hit the balls through the covered wagons.

Food

Trail Mix

Mix in a large mixing
  bowl:

1 cup of Wheat Chex®

1 cup of Rice Chex®

1 cup of raisins

1 cup of peanuts

1 cup of pretzel sticks

$1/2$ cup of pumpkin
  seeds

Pigs in a Blanket

Give each child one
uncooked biscuit from a
can and one Vienna
sausage. Show the
children how to wrap
their biscuits around the
sausages. Place on an
ungreased cookie sheet,
and bake for 10 minutes.

Chips

Serve corn chips or
another favorite chip
variety from your local
grocery store.

Trail Mix

Chips

Pigs in a Blanket

Hot Chocolate

Mix 1 tablespoon of chocolate syrup with 8 ounces of milk and heat. Be sure to add a marshmallow.

Wagon Wheel Cookies

Give each child a small bowl of refrigerated peanut butter cookie dough, and tell them to shape it into a circle. Show the children how to make wagon wheel spokes by using a craft stick to make indentations. Bake as directed on the package.

Hot Chocolate

Wagon Wheel Cookies

Favors and Frills

Favors

Bandannas (can be purchased inexpensively from a fabric store or dime store)

Cowboy/cowgirl hats (use the pattern in the Frills section)

Stick horses used in the Fun section

Frills

Cowboy Decor
Decorate the room or yard with cowboy hats, ropes, bandannas, and boots.

Branding Iron Designs
Use branding iron designs on the walls and tables.

Campfire
Create a campfire with empty paper towel tubes (or real sticks and small limbs) and red and yellow tissue paper. Crumple the paper and lay the tubes or sticks over it. Pull the ends of the paper through the sticks so that they look like flames.

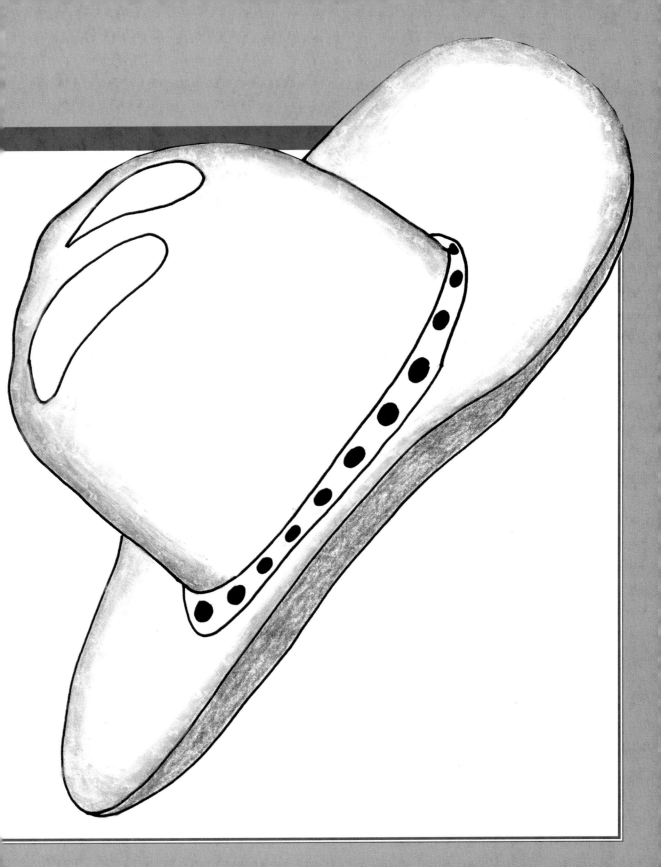

Facts

Chuck wagons were like rolling kitchens that

followed cowhands on a cattle drive. The name

came from the slang word *chuck*, meaning food.

Cow "patties" (dried manure) were often used as

kindling for campfires.

Cowboys used the campfire to keep wild animals

away from camp.

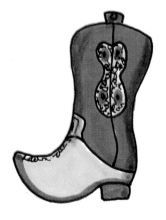

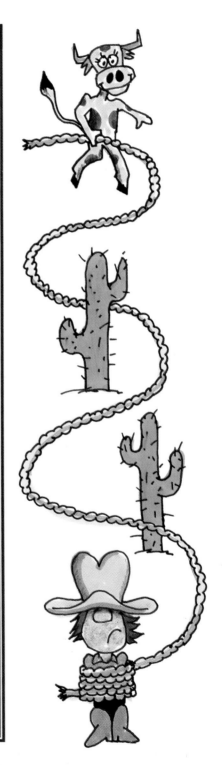

R O U N D U P

Grossman, Virginia. *Ten Little Rabbits.* Chronicle, 1991. This counting book celebrates Native American traditions, such as weaving, fishing, and storytelling.

⋯⋯⋯⋯⋯⋯⋯⋯⋯⋯⋯⋯⋯⋯⋯⋯⋯⋯⋯⋯

McDermott, Gerald. *Coyote: A Trickster Tale from the Southwest.* Harcourt, 1992. This tale of a wily coyote was inspired by Zuni folklore.

⋯⋯⋯⋯⋯⋯⋯⋯⋯⋯⋯⋯⋯⋯⋯⋯⋯⋯⋯⋯

Martin, Bill, Jr., and John Archambault. *Knots on a Counting Rope.* Holt, 1987. A grandfather tells the story of his grandson's life while tying a knot on a counting rope for each event.

⋯⋯⋯⋯⋯⋯⋯⋯⋯⋯⋯⋯⋯⋯⋯⋯⋯⋯⋯⋯

Martin, Bill, Jr., and John Archambault. *Barn Dance!* Holt, 1986. A group of animals throws a dance in the middle of the night.

HOLIDAY PARTIES

Harvest Party

Pumpkins,
scarecrows,
everywhere!

Bright colored
leaves and cool,
crisp air.

At the Harvest
Party we will share

the fun of Autumn,
so please be there!

FanFare

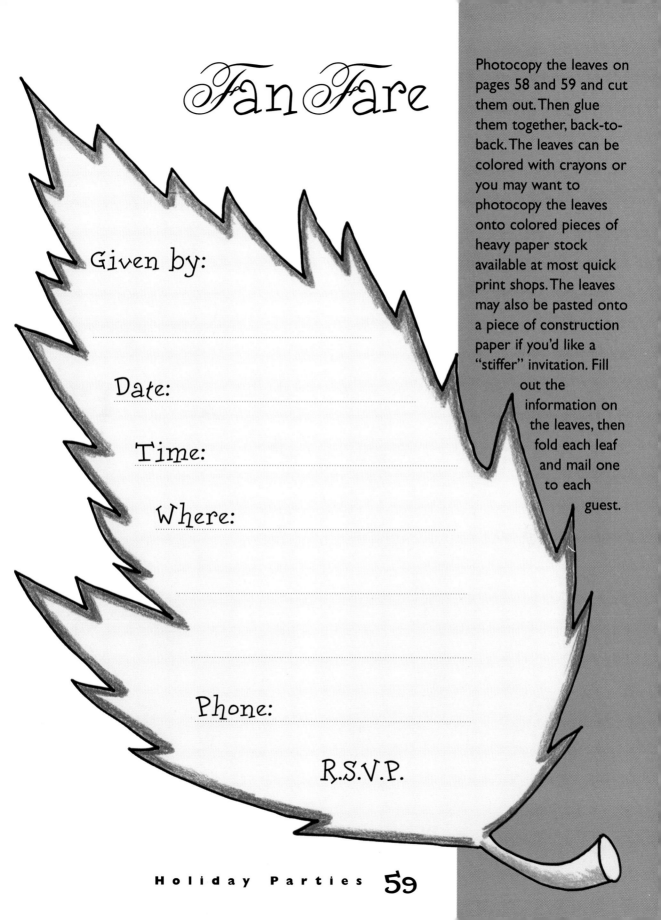

Given by:

....

Date: ....

Time: ....

Where:

....

....

Phone: ....

R.S.V.P.

Photocopy the leaves on pages 58 and 59 and cut them out. Then glue them together, back-to-back. The leaves can be colored with crayons or you may want to photocopy the leaves onto colored pieces of heavy paper stock available at most quick print shops. The leaves may also be pasted onto a piece of construction paper if you'd like a "stiffer" invitation. Fill out the information on the leaves, then fold each leaf and mail one to each guest.

Harvest Party

Pumpkin Painting

Give the children paints and a small pumpkin each. Encourage them to paint their pumpkins any way they like.

Pumpkin Toss

Cut a large pumpkin from a piece of orange posterboard, and paint eyes and a nose on it. Glue or tape the jack-o'-lantern to the side of a box. Cut out a 6" circle for the mouth. Let the children take turns tossing beanbags or Ping Pong balls through the mouth.

Pin the Nose on the Pumpkin

Cut a big pumpkin shape out of orange posterboard or bulletin board paper (available at teacher supply stores). Use black construction paper to make the eyes, mouth, and nose. Glue the eyes and mouth in place. Put fun tack or sticky putty on the nose. Let the children take turns trying to put the nose in the right place while they are blindfolded.

Pumpkin Rolling Relay

Divide the children into two teams, and stand them in two lines. Mark a starting line and a turnaround line (about 20' apart) on the floor or the ground. Have the first child in each line roll a pumpkin from the starting line to the turnaround line, and then back to the starting line. The next teammate in line repeats the pattern. The first team to have everyone complete the course wins.

Pumpkin Concentration

Get twelve circular pizza boards (from a pizza parlor) or cake boards (from a craft store). Paint the boards to look like jack-o'-lanterns, creating six matching pairs. Put the boards face down on the floor. One at a time, the children turn over one board and then choose another board, turn it over, and see if it matches the first one. When a child misses, the turn goes to the next child. A match gets another turn.

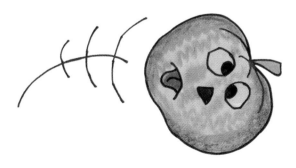

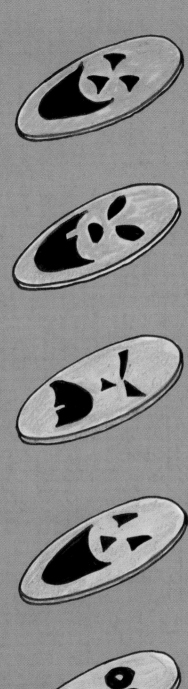

𝓕ood

Pumpkin Punch

Make a punch bowl out of a large pumpkin. Cut the top off, spoon out the meat, and scrape the sides. Fill with vanilla ice cream and ginger ale.

Pumpkin
Punch

62

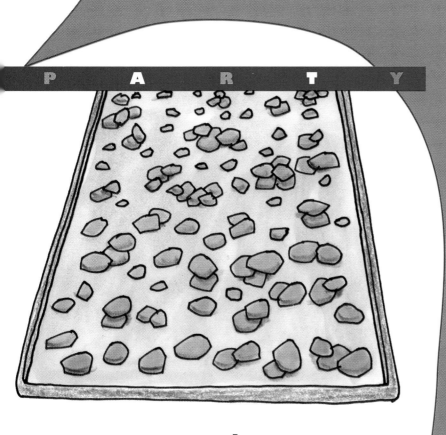

Toasted Pumpkin Seeds

Miniature
Pumpkin
Pies

Miniature Pumpkin Pies

Give each child a paper cupcake holder. Have children place a vanilla wafer in the bottom of their cups and then fill with pumpkin pie filling (prepared as directed on the can). Top with miniature marshmallows, and bake for 10 minutes at 375°.

Toasted Pumpkin Seeds

Clean the seeds you removed from the pumpkin punch bowl. Place them on a greased cookie sheet, and toast for 8 minutes, turning them once or twice.

Favors and Frills

Favors

Painted pumpkins from the Fun section

Frills

Make a **scarecrow** by stuffing clothes with crumpled newspapers. Set out your scarecrow to greet guests when they arrive.

Decorate the room or yard with paper cutout **pumpkins** and **cornstalks**.

Seat your guests on **bales of hay**.

Facts

H A R V E S T

Most cultures celebrate the harvest. In the United States, we have Thanksgiving Day.

Harvest days celebrate gathering the fall crops and putting them up for winter.

The most popular crops of harvest days are gourds, pumpkins, and corn.

Fiction

Aesop. "The Ant and the Grasshopper." Many versions available. In this well-known fable, the grasshopper spends his time playing while the ant works to store food for the long, cold winter.

Ehlert, Lois. *Red Leaf, Yellow Leaf.* Harcourt, 1991. A maple seed takes root in a forest, nursery workers harvest it, and a little girl plants it in her yard.

Rockwell, Anne. *Apples and Pumpkins.* Macmillan, 1989. A girl and her family pick apples and pumpkins for Halloween.

Sobol, Harriet, and Patricia Agre. *A Book of Vegetables*. Dodd, 1984. This book of photographs shows a variety of plants from blossom time to harvest time.

Titherington, Jeanne. *Pumpkin Pumpkin.* Greenwillow, 1986. A toddler named Jamie helps keep alive the growing cycle of a pumpkin patch.

Bring Your Own Booth
CARNIVAL

Photocopy the front and back of the invitation. Cut out both tent shapes and glue them back-to-back. For a sturdier invitation, "sandwich" a piece of construction paper between the two cutouts and glue all three pieces together.

Photocopy "tickets" from pages 70 through 73. Cut each one out and include one "ticket" with each invitation. These "tickets" explain to the parents of the guests what "booth" each guest is asked to bring to the party. Expect a few phone calls from parents who have questions. Encourage parents to keep it simple and fun.

Come to The
CARNIVAL PARTY

PARTY

Given by: _____

Date: _____

Time: _____

Where: _____

_____

Phone: _____   R.S.V.P.

Each guest is asked to bring a "Booth" to this party. Information on the booth we'd like YOU to bring is attached. Call if you have questions.

The following are booths with games to be played at the backyard carnival:

Duck Pond

Digging for Gold

Beanbag Toss

Fishing Pond

Cake Walk

Penny Toss

Bowling

Paper Airplane Toss

Collapse the Cans

You'll need lots of help with this party. Ask parents and friends to work the booths so that children will be free to play.

Host provides prizes.

Bring Your Own Booth

F U N   F U   F U

Duck Pond Booth

TICKET

What you'll need to bring for your booth:

- Plastic tub big enough to float three ducks

- Three floating plastic ducks, each with a different colored dot attached to the bottom so it won't come off in water.

How to set up and operate your booth:

Fill the tub with enough water to float the ducks. The players select a duck and are awarded a prize dependent upon the color they draw.

Digging for Gold

TICKET

What you'll need to bring for your booth:

- Plastic tub filled with sand with pennies buried in it.

- Strainer with large holes.

How to set up and operate your booth:

The children use the strainer to dig a scoop of sand and are allowed to keep the pennies that remain in the strainer after the sand sifts through.

Carnival Party

Fishing Pond

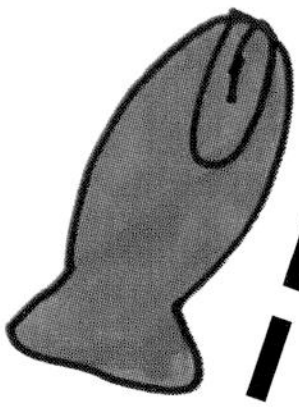

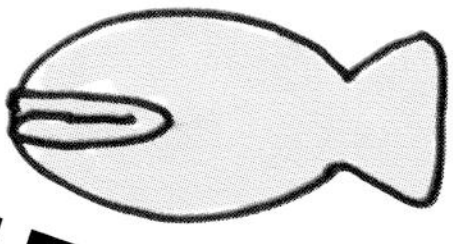

TICKET

What you'll need to bring for your booth:

- Shallow pan
- Colored paper fish (about 4" long with a paper clip attached to the nose)
- Fishing pole made from a short dowel, yarn, and a magnet for a hook.

How to set up and operate your booth:

The children catch the fish by touching the magnet to the paper clip on the fish's nose. Prizes are awarded according to the color of fish caught.

Cake Walk

TICKET

What you'll need to bring for your booth:

- I' square pieces of colored paper, cardboard, or carpet squares
- Cassette player and tapes

How to set up and operate your booth:

Arrange paper, cardboard, or carpet squares into a circle. Mark an "X" on a few of the squares. As the music plays, the children walk around the circle. When the music stops, children on squares marked with an "X" get a special prize. Other children get alternative prizes.

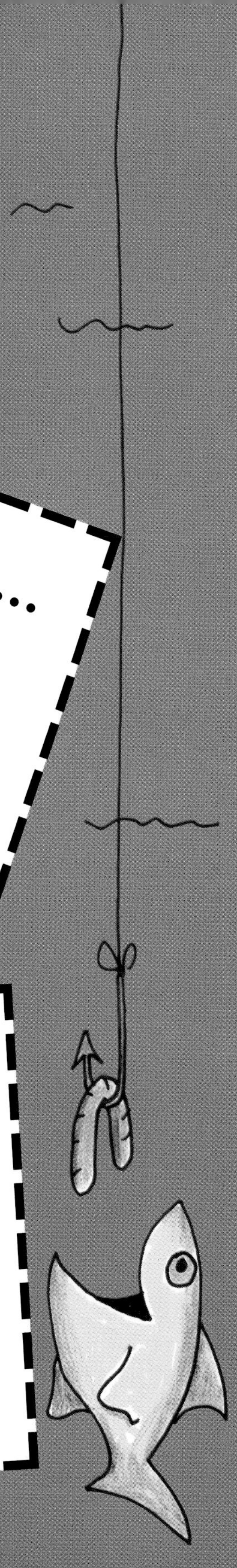

71

FUN FUN FU

Collapse the Cans

What you'll need to bring for your booth:

- Three empty soft drink cans
- Small stool
- Tennis balls

How to set up and operate your booth:

Stack the cans in a pyramid shape on the stool. The children toss one or more tennis balls and try to knock down the cans.

TICKET

Penny Toss Booth

What you'll need to bring for your booth:

- Four saucers
- Four pennies

How to set up and operate your booth:

The children attempt to toss pennies into the saucers and get them to stay.

TICKET

Bowling Booth

TICKET

What you'll need to bring for your booth:

- Ten toilet paper or paper towel tubes
- Tennis balls

How to set up and operate your booth:

Stand the tubes upright on the ground, and give each player a tennis ball. The children see how many tubes they can knock down by rolling the ball, as in bowling.

Paper Airplane Toss

TICKET

What you'll need to bring for your booth:

- Hula Hoop®
- Paper airplanes (constructed by adults prior to the party)

How to set up and operate your booth:

Suspend the Hula Hoop® from overhead (from a tree or the eaves of the house) with string. The children take turns trying to toss paper airplanes through the hoop.

Beanbag Toss

TICKET

What you'll need to bring for your booth:

- Decorated box
- Beanbags (or table tennis balls)

How to set up and operate your booth:

The children see how many beanbags they can toss into the box.

Food

C A R N I V A L

Popcorn

Pop popcorn in the regular way. Then offer children a variety of seasonings to "spice it up." Cinnamon and sugar, seasoned salt, and parmesan cheese all make great seasonings.

Popcorn

Cookie Decorating

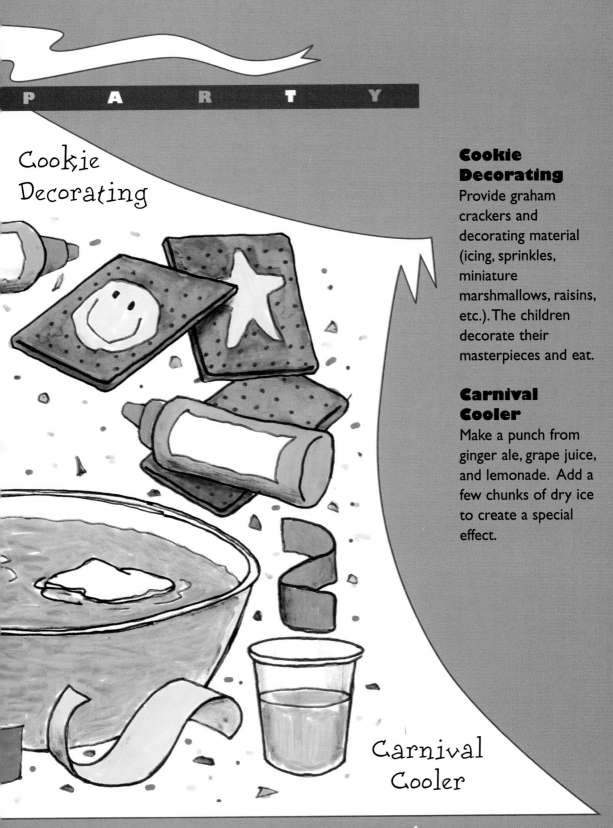

Cookie Decorating

Provide graham crackers and decorating material (icing, sprinkles, miniature marshmallows, raisins, etc.). The children decorate their masterpieces and eat.

Carnival Cooler

Make a punch from ginger ale, grape juice, and lemonade. Add a few chunks of dry ice to create a special effect.

Carnival Cooler

Favors and Frills

Favors

Stickers
(available at discount stores)

Coupons
Local fast-food restaurants will often donate a small number of "freebie" or discount coupons for children's parties. Check with local movie theaters too. Contact the manager.

Small plastic toys
Bathtub toys, small boxes of chalk, doodle pads, and pencils make great favors.

Frills

Ticket Booth
Get a discarded cardboard refrigerator box from a local appliance store. Cut a "window" in the box, and write the words "Ticket Booth" over the window. Inside, the guest of honor takes "tickets." Each guest's "ticket" is the invitation to the party. Of course, this is just for fun, and no ticket is necessary for admittance.

The Big Top
If you have a tentlike structure that you take to the beach to protect you from the sun, you can use it to set up some booths under the tent.

Indoor Big Top
Drape blue and yellow crêpe paper from the center of a room toward each corner to give a "tent" look.

Facts

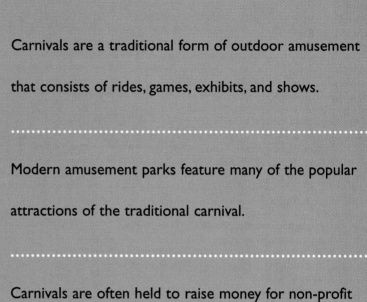

Carnivals are a traditional form of outdoor amusement that consists of rides, games, exhibits, and shows.

Modern amusement parks feature many of the popular attractions of the traditional carnival.

Carnivals are often held to raise money for non-profit agencies and organizations, such as the Muscular Dystrophy Association.

There are more than 500 carnivals that travel across the United States.

The carousel and Ferris wheel are the most popular carnival rides.

Fiction

Crews, Donald. *Carousel.* Greenwillow, 1982.

Wonderful illustrations depict a whirling carousel ride.

Dorros, Arthur. *Tonight Is Carnival.* Dutton, 1991.

This is the story of a Puerto Rican Carnival.

Martin, Bill Jr., and John Archambault. *Merry Go Round.*

Holt, 1990. This is a poetic description of a

merry-go-round.

Best Buddies

BRING a Buddy

to a
Best Buddy
Party!

Party

Fan-Fare

Given by:

....

Date:

....

Time:

....

Where:

....

....

....

Phone:

....

R.S.V.P.

Photocopy the two hands and color the front. Cut out both hands and glue them back-to-back. For a sturdier invitation, "sandwich" a piece of construction paper between the two hand cutouts and glue all three pieces together. Place invitations into envelopes and mail to each guest.

Best Buddies Party

Friendship Bracelets

Give each child a 2' length of yarn. Encourage the children to finger crochet, braid, or twist a bracelet for a friend.

Heart-Shaped Stick Puppets

Let the children decorate construction-paper hearts and glue them to tongue depressors to make stick puppets (see illustration).

Three-Legged Race

Have each pair of buddies stand side by side. Tie their touching legs together at the ankles with a piece of hosiery. Let the children race.

Make a funny face!

Sing a song!

Pick a Heart
Use the pictures on this page to create a set of cards. Photocopy them, cut them out, and glue them to the back of heart-shaped pieces of construction paper. Let each child pick a heart and follow the directions.

Stand on your head!

Snap your fingers!

Walk with a book on your head!

Make some animal sounds!

BARK
OINK
BAA

Touch your toes!

Close your eyes, touch your nose!

Rub your head, pat your tummy!

Stand on one foot!

Food

Friendship Salad

Cream Cheese Heart.

Friendship Salad

Have each child bring a piece of fruit to the party. Let the children help peel and cut the fruit to make a salad. Use salad dressing, whipped cream, or yogurt to mix the salad. Core an apple for each child, and let the children fill their apples with the salad.

Cream Cheese Hearts

Blend 2 tablespoons of cherry juice with 8 ounces of cream cheese. Use a heart-shaped cookie cutter to cut hearts from slices of bread. Spread the cherry cream cheese on the bread hearts. Decorate them with cherry halves.

84

Crispy
Hearts

Red
Hots

Crispy Hearts

Use canned biscuits. Shape each one into a heart, and brush with butter. Sprinkle with a cinnamon and sugar mixture, and bake as instructed on the can.

Red Hots

Purchase cinnamon-flavored candy pieces from your local grocery or candy store.

85

Favors

Friendship bracelets from the Fun section.

Heart-shaped stick puppets from the Fun section.

Pen Pal Envelopes
Each child writes his or her address (adults help, of course) on an envelope (provided by the host or hostess). Best buddies exchange envelopes and bring them home after the party. Later everyone writes a pen pal letter to his or her best buddy. Letters can include drawings of best buddies doing something together.

Huge Heart

Take an old white bed sheet and dye it pink. Cut from it a large heart-shaped piece. Use pushpins to place the heart over the front door.

Photo Backdrop

Make a large sign that says "Best Buddies." Have each set of buddies stand in front of the sign while the host takes a photograph of them together. When developing the prints, have double prints made, and send a print to each of the buddies.

Buddie Chains

Using freezer wrap or other "rolled" paper, cut a long row of paper dolls with arms connected. Attach string to each end, and drape from the ceiling or hang it on the walls. Be sure to make "girl" and "boy" dolls if your party has both genders attending.

Facts

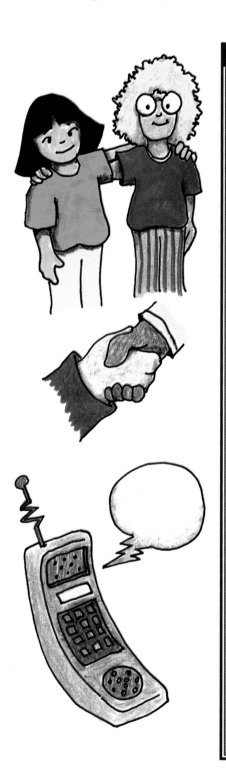

Some best buddies are well known to everyone. Ask children to name as many as they can (such as Tom and Jerry, Snoopy and Woodstock, Garfield the cat and Odie the dog—or maybe Jon, Garfield's owner).

Some best buddies live far apart and communicate by letters, phones, and computers.

The world congress established an International Friendship Day. It is celebrated on August 4.

In the United States, people consider Valentine's Day a friendship day.

Fiction

Cohen, Miriam. *Best Friends*. Macmillan, 1989.
Jim knows that Paul is his best friend. A day at school
causes Jim to have some doubts, but when an emergency
occurs, all doubt disappears.

Hallinan, P. K. *That's What A Friend Is*. Ideals, 1985.
Every page of this book helps children understand
the meaning of friendship.

Heine, Helme. *Friends*. Macmillan, 1982. This story
about a rooster, a mouse, and a pig includes all the
important elements of friendship.

Henkes, Kevin. *Chester's Way*. Greenwillow, 1988.
Chester and his best friend Wilson do everything
together. They are so much alike that they only have to
make one Christmas list. Then Lilly moves into the
neighborhood.

Kellogg, Steven. *Best Friends*. Dial, 1986. Kathy and
Louise are best friends. Louise goes away for the
summer, and Kathy learns a valuable lesson about
friendship.

Fourth of July

You're invited to a

Fourth of July

Splash Day Party!

Photocopy the two hotdogs and color them. Cut out both hot dog pieces and glue them back-to-back. For a sturdier invitation, "sandwich" a piece of construction paper between the two hotdog cutouts and glue all three pieces together.

Splash Day

This party is being given by

Date:

Time:

Where:

Phone:

Bring a bathing suit!

Your local "quick print" shop will probably also have heavier weight sheets of colored paper onto which you can photocopy the hotdog drawings if you want to eliminate the coloring step. Place invitations into envelopes and mail to each guest.

Fourth of July

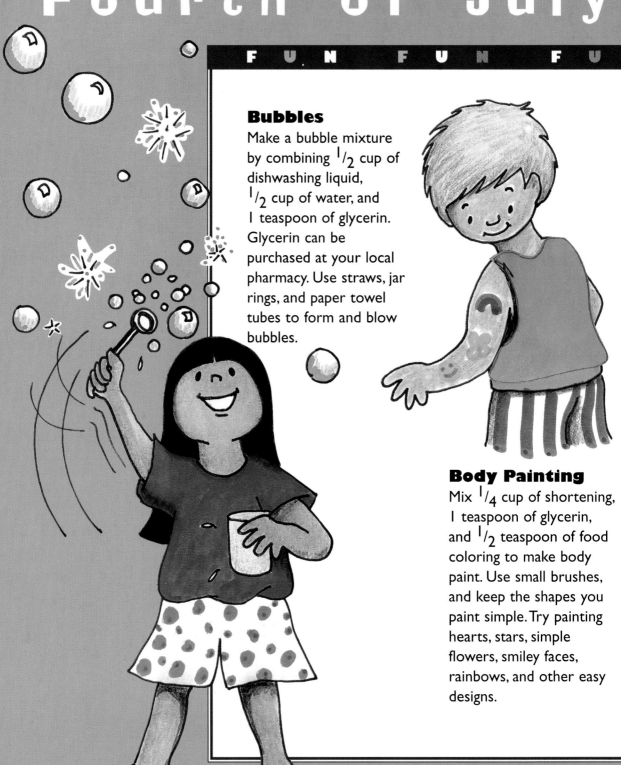

Bubbles

Make a bubble mixture by combining $1/2$ cup of dishwashing liquid, $1/2$ cup of water, and 1 teaspoon of glycerin. Glycerin can be purchased at your local pharmacy. Use straws, jar rings, and paper towel tubes to form and blow bubbles.

Body Painting

Mix $1/4$ cup of shortening, 1 teaspoon of glycerin, and $1/2$ teaspoon of food coloring to make body paint. Use small brushes, and keep the shapes you paint simple. Try painting hearts, stars, simple flowers, smiley faces, rainbows, and other easy designs.

Splash Day

Squirt Painting

Fill squirt bottles with liquid tempera paint (available at most discount stores and all art supply stores) and a teaspoon of liquid detergent. Provide a large sheet of butcher paper or newsprint for children to squirt paint.

Clothes Washing/ Furniture Washing

Children love to wash things. Give them a pail of soapy water and some doll clothes or plastic furniture to wash.

More Fun

Sprinkler Play

Turn on the sprinkler, and let the children run in the mist.

Mud Pies

All you need is a mud puddle, some pots and pans, and children. Provide acorns, leaves, bark, and rocks for decorating.

Water Balloon Toss

Fill balloons with water and let children toss them into plastic laundry baskets or boxes.

Footprint Mural

Put liquid tempera paint in a shallow cake pan. Encourage the children to take off their shoes, step in the paint, and walk down a strip of butcher paper. Be sure to have a tub of soapy water and a towel waiting at the other end of the paper.

Food

Watermelon on a Stick

Mix 1 cup of seedless watermelon pieces, 1 cup of orange juice, and 1 cup of water. Pour the mixture in small paper cups, and set them in the freezer. Insert Popsicle® sticks when the mixture is partially frozen. A piece of clear plastic wrap placed over the cup will help hold the Popsicle® stick in place. Finish freezing.

Snow Cones

Put crushed ice in snow-cone cups. Let the children top them with flavored syrups. (Put syrups in pump bottles.)

Watermelon on a Stick

Snow Cones

96

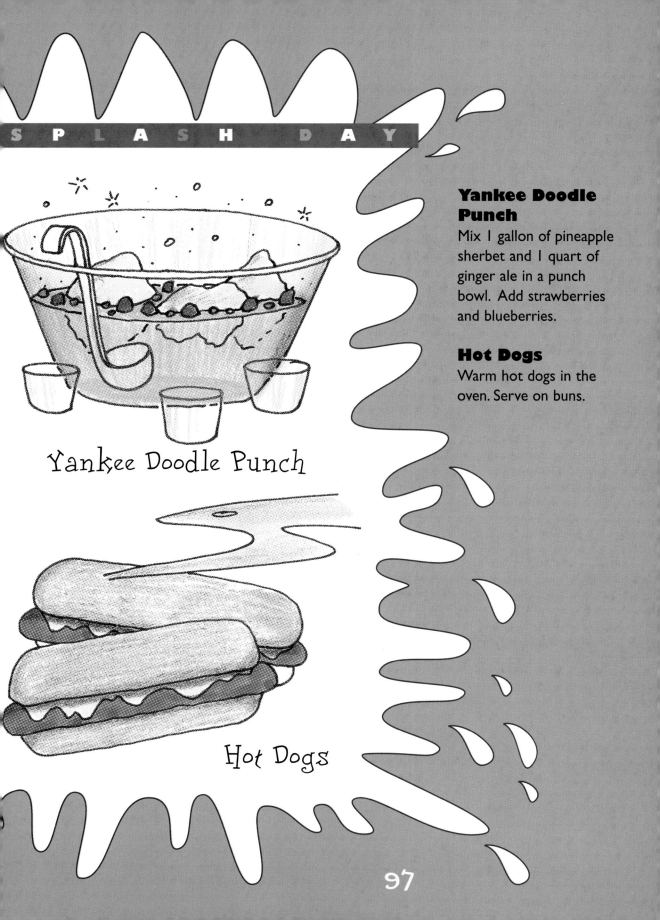

Yankee Doodle Punch

Hot Dogs

Yankee Doodle Punch

Mix 1 gallon of pineapple sherbet and 1 quart of ginger ale in a punch bowl. Add strawberries and blueberries.

Hot Dogs

Warm hot dogs in the oven. Serve on buns.

Favors

Small bottles of **bubbles** with bubble wands

Small American **flags**

Red, white, and blue **lollipops**

"Firecracker" **coloring sheet** (see illustration on page 95)

Frills

Streamers and Balloons
Decorate the room or yard with red, white, and blue streamers and balloons. Include some Christmas tree tinsel too.

Red, White, and Blue Table
Use red, white, and blue cups, plates, and napkins.

Marching Music
Borrow a tape or CD of patriotic marches from the library. Play the music as the guests enter.

Water Toys
Decorate the room or yard with water toys, such as plastic boats, floats, and bathtub toys. Seat guests on inner tubes or other swimming pool floats.

The Fourth of July is the birthday of the United States. It marks the day the Declaration of Independence was adopted.

The first Independence Day celebration was held in Philadelphia.

People all over the country celebrate the Fourth of July with parades, shows, fireworks, marching bands, and food.

Facts

Fiction

Bangs, Edward. *Yankee Doodle.* Macmillan, 1989. This richly illustrated story uses the song "Yankee Doodle" as a theme.

Brown, Marcia. *Stone Soup.* Macmillan, 1979. Three soldiers outwit some selfish villagers, and everyone profits.

Kherdian, David, and Nonny Hogrogian. *The Cat's Midsummer Jamboree.* Philomel, 1990. A roaming mandolin-playing cat encounters a number of other musical animals on his travels, and the result is a jamboree in a tree.

Spier, Peter. *Crash! Bang! Boom!* Doubleday, 1990. This colorful parade is complete with marching and all the sound effects.

Van Rynback, Iris. *The Stone Soup.* Greenwillow, 1988. A Revolutionary War soldier outsmarts a village of selfish people, and everyone benefits. This story is similar to the Marcia Brown version but has different illustrations and some minor character changes.

Just for Fun
PARTIES

Come As You Are

Photocopy the front and back of the invitations and color them. Cut out both pieces and glue them back-to-back. For a sturdier invitation, "sandwich" a piece of construction paper between the front and back and glue all three pieces together.

You're invited to a

Come As You Are Breakfast

Breakfast Fan-Fare

Your local "quick print" shop will probably have heavier weight sheets of colored paper onto which you can photocopy the invitations if you want to eliminate the coloring step. Place invitations into envelopes and mail to each guest.

This party is being given by

Date:

Time:

Where:

Phone:

Come As You Are

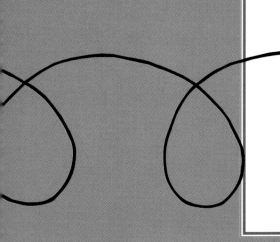

Wee Sing Silly Songs

If you are going to be driving to pick up party guests, take along the cassette tape *Wee Sing Silly Songs* by Pamela Conn Beall and Susan Hagen Nipp (Price Stern Sloan, 1986). This will help get everyone awake and cheery. Children will love singing along, and you will appreciate the entertainment.

Happy Face Relay

Paint two circular pizza or cake boards, and draw happy faces on them with a marker. Mark a starting line and a turnaround line on the floor or ground. Divide the children into two teams, and stage a relay race with the children rolling the happy faces as they run.

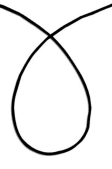
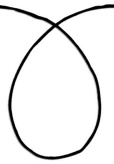

Breakfast

Pin the Smile on the Sunshine

Cut a circle 3' in diameter from yellow bulletin board paper (available at teacher supply stores). Draw eyes and a nose on the circle with a marker. Cut a smiling mouth from black construction paper, and put a small piece of sticky putty on the back. Let the children take turns trying to put the mouth in the right place while blindfolded.

Alarm Clock Toss

Get two service counter bells (available at office supply stores). Draw clock faces on two 6" paper plates. Punch a small hole in the center of each plate, and place the plates over the knobs on the bells. Have the children stand 4" to 6" from the bell and toss a beanbag to ring the bell. Those children who are successful may then try to hit the bell again from a greater distance. The child who can hit the bell from the greatest distance wins the game.

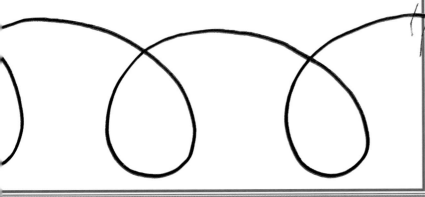

Food

Happy Face Pancakes

On a hot pan or griddle, pour 2 drops of pancake batter for eyes and a half-moon of batter for a mouth. Let cook 40 seconds, and then pour enough batter over it to make a regular-sized pancake. Finish cooking. Serve face-up.

Orange Delights

Beat or blend two eggs or $1/4$ cup egg substitute into a quart of orange juice and serve over ice.

Happy Face Pancakes

Orange Delights

Bananas
on a
Stick

Bananas on a Stick

Peel bananas, and cut them in half, crosswise. Place each half on a Popsicle® stick, and freeze. When ready to serve, provide chocolate syrup, honey, yogurt, and peanut butter for the children to dip their bananas into.

Favors and Frills

Favors

Happy Face Refrigerator Magnets
Use the patterns from the Frills section or plastic milk jug lids. Glue a $1/2$" magnetic strip (available at craft stores) to the back of each cutout. Paint the circles yellow. Let the children draw happy faces on them.

Frills

Faces
Make clock faces and sunshine faces. Hang them from the ceiling with monofilament or tape them to the walls.

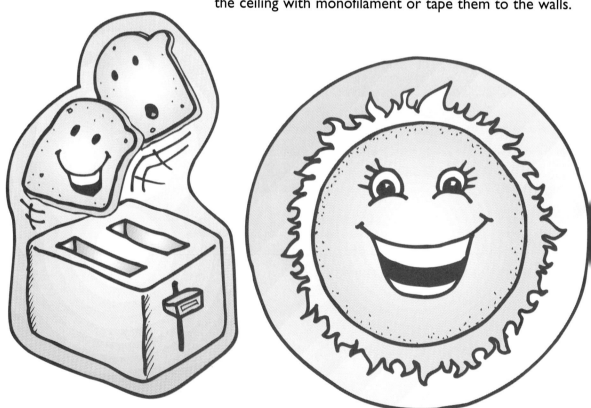

Facts

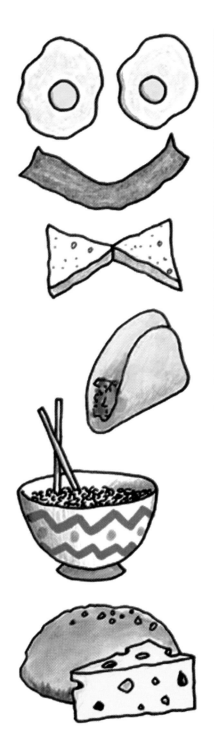

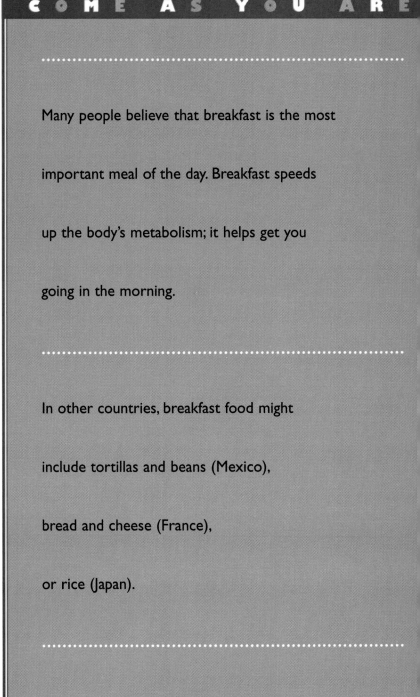

Many people believe that breakfast is the most

important meal of the day. Breakfast speeds

up the body's metabolism; it helps get you

going in the morning.

In other countries, breakfast food might

include tortillas and beans (Mexico),

bread and cheese (France),

or rice (Japan).

Fiction

Dryden, Emma. *Good Morning, Good Night.* Random House, 1990. Romp through morning routines with six furry animals.

Field, Eugene. *Wynken, Blynken, and Nod.* Putnam, 1986. This is the wonderful poem about three sleepy children sailing in a sea of stars.

Ginsburg, Mirra. *Good Morning, Chick.* Greenwillow, 1980. The barnyard wakes up in this simple, beautifully illustrated book.

Ormerod, Jan. *Sunshine.* Lothrop, 1981. This wordless picture book chronicles the start of a little girl's day.

Wood, Audrey. *The Napping House.* Harcourt, 1984. This is a cumulative tale of a house where everyone is peacefully sleeping until a flea bites the cat and starts a chain reaction.

Wacky WEDNESDAY Party

Below are a number of ideas for *Wacky Wednesday invitations.*

Note: *On the invitation, suggest that everyone wear one wacky thing, such as a coat that's too big, swim fins, or a cowboy hat with a feather.*

Before throwing a "Wacky Wednesday" party, read the children's book "Wacky Wednesday" by Theo LeSieg.

Balloon Invitation

Inflate a balloon and write all the information about the party (time, date, etc.) on the balloon with a paint pen or permanent marker. Now, deflate the balloon, put it in an envelope, and mail it to a guest. Do the same for each guest.

PLEASE COME TO MY WACKY WEDNESDAY PARTY.

Backwards Invitation

Send an invitation on which the information is written backwards, so each guest will have to look in a mirror to read it.

Tube Invitation

Assist the child who is giving the party in drawing an invitation on a sheet of unlined 8$\frac{1}{2}$" by 11" paper. Photocopy enough invitations for each guest. Then have the child add some bright colors to each invitation using markers and/or crayons. Roll up the invitation and insert it in a paper towel tube. Put some confetti, glitter, and curly pieces of ribbon inside. Wrap the tube with brown paper, address it, and mail it to a guest. Make one tube for each of the other guests.

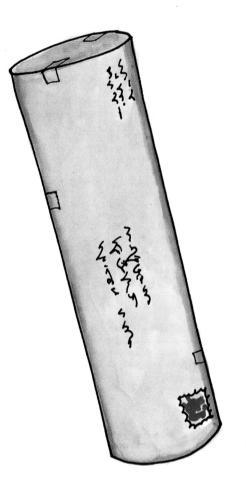

Inside-Outside Invitation

Write all the information about the party (time, date, etc.) on the outside of the envelope, along with the address. Inside the envelope, put a slip of paper that says, "Hope you can join us!"

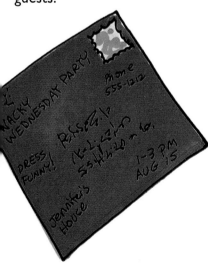

Fan-Fare

or

how to *invite* everybody to the party!

Wacky WEDNESDAY Party

Wacky Wednesday

Wacky Beads

Hang pieces of yarn from the ceiling or the limb of a tree. Encourage the children to string beads up, instead of the usual way.

Wacky Thing Search

Arrange household items in strange positions and place typical household items in strange places. For example, turn the television toward the wall, place a bar of soap on the coffee table, stick a fly swatter in a flower vase, set a hammer in the bathtub, and so on. Challenge the children to find all of the wacky things.

Party

Wacky Drawings

Tape pieces of drawing
paper to the underside
of low tables or chairs.
Have each child lie on
his or her back and draw
a picture.

More Fun

Wacky Clothes Contest

Have the children show off their wacky clothes. Give prizes for the most colorful, the silliest, the most original, and the most backward.

Wacky Face Contest

Give everyone a turn to make the wackiest, funniest face he or she can make. Parents can assist with simple makeup if they'd like. Take Polaroid® photos of the funny faces, and display them on a piece of posterboard. Have the children vote on the wackiest face.

Wacky People Collage

Ahead of time, cut out parts of faces from photos in old newspapers and magazines. Give each child a piece of paper with a large circle drawn on it, and hand each child an assortment of face "pieces." Have them glue the pieces onto the paper and make wacky people collages.

Food

Inside-Out Sandwiches

Make peanut butter and jelly sandwiches with the peanut butter and jelly on the outside of the bread.

Crazy Chips

Mix grapes and raisins with your favorite chips.

Inside-Out Sandwiches

Crazy Chips

Two-Tone
Fruit
Juice

Upside-Down
Cake

Two-Tone Fruit Juice

Pour each child's glass half-full of concentrated Hawaiian Punch®, and then fill it with orange juice. The Hawaiian Punch® is thicker and will stay on the bottom, creating a two-toned effect.

Upside-Down Cake

Stick the candles in the side of the cake, instead of on top.

Favors

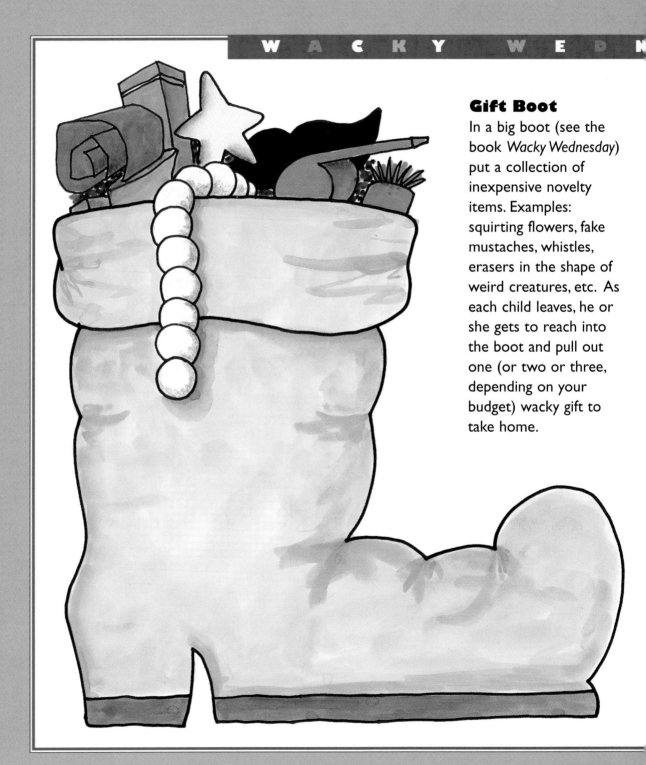

Gift Boot

In a big boot (see the book *Wacky Wednesday*) put a collection of inexpensive novelty items. Examples: squirting flowers, fake mustaches, whistles, erasers in the shape of weird creatures, etc. As each child leaves, he or she gets to reach into the boot and pull out one (or two or three, depending on your budget) wacky gift to take home.

Wacky Entrance

Have the guests enter in some unusual way. For example, have them enter through a low window, crawl through a "tunnel" or maze of cardboard boxes, or go through an outdoor obstacle course before entering.

Wacky Body

Cover the front of a large cardboard box with butcher paper. Draw the body of a funny animal, a space creature, or an object (such as a playing card) on the front of the box. Cut a hole large enough for a child to stick his or her head through. Encourage the children to take turns sticking their heads in the hole and then watching as their friends do the same.

Wacky Video

If you have a video camera, set it up near the door and put a portable television set next to the camera. Whether you are recording or not, point the camera so that the children can see themselves in the television screen. Encourage them to make funny faces.

Facts

Doing something backwards is a good way to tell how well one understands a task.

Two good places to find wacky facts are *Ripley's Believe It or Not* and the *Guiness Book of Records*. There are records for almost everything including pogo stick jumping, cutting the longest apple peel, doing the largest number of high kicks, playing drums for the longest number of hours, fastest slicing of a cucumber, and most number of hands shaken. Many of the records are broken each year.

Fiction

Browne, Anthony. *Changes*. Knopf, 1990. When a little boy's father tells him there are going to be some changes, the boy imagines all kinds of wacky things. He is almost relieved to find out that the change his father is talking about is a new baby.

Gackenbach, Dick. *King Wacky*. Crown, 1984. A king has his head on backwards, which really changes the way things look.

Krauss, Ruth. *The Backward Day*. Harper, 1950. A boy spends a backward day, doing such things as wearing his clothes over his coat, walking backwards, and saying "Good night" in the morning.

LeSieg, Theo. *Wacky Wednesday*. Beginner Books, 1974. This counting book is filled with absurdities, such as a jet in freeway traffic and a mouse chasing a cat.

Junior DETECTIVE Party

Fill out the Junior Detective Party invitation (see page 125). Reduce the size of the invitation by photocopying it several times at maximum reduction. Include in the invitation an inexpensive plastic magnifying glass, available at most toy or party stores. Mail the invitation and magnifying glass in the smallest envelopes you can find.

IMPORTANT SECRET MESSAGE!

THERE WILL BE A PARTY FOR YOU AND OTHER JUNIOR DETECTIVES AT THE TIME AND PLACE SHOWN BELOW. BE PREPARED FOR A TREASURE HUNT, GUESSING GAMES, AND MYSTERY SNACKS. THE "PASSWORD" IS YOUR NAME.

CHIEF DETECTIVE:

HEADQUARTERS ADDRESS:

DATE: HOURS:

SECRET PHONE NUMBER:

Fan-Fare

or

how to

invite

everybody

to the

party!

Junior Detective

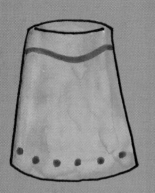

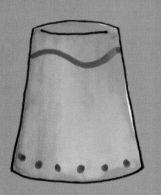

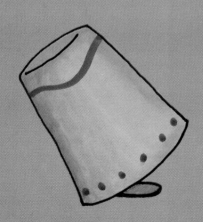

Which Cup Hides the Stone?

Hide a stone under one of three cups turned upside down on a table. Move the cups around and let the children guess which cup hides the stone.

Pass the Penny

Choose one child to be "It." Ask "It" to leave the room. Have the other children sit in a circle. Choose one child to be the Penny Holder. When "It" returns, the other children pass a penny around the circle. When the penny gets to the Penny Holder, he or she keeps it while the others pretend to keep passing it. "Its" job is to guess who has the penny. Once "It" guesses correctly the Penny Holder becomes the new "It," and the game starts again.

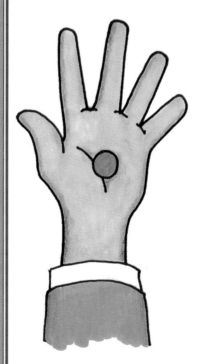

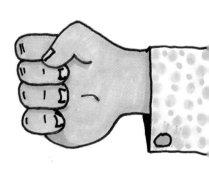

Party

Treasure Hunt

Set up a Treasure Hunt. Hide prizes or favors, and let the children solve riddles to find them. Here are some possible clues:

It's under a place where you sit. (chair)

It's in a cold place. (freezer or refrigerator)

It's under a place where you wipe your feet. (door mat or bath mat)

It's in a place that gets very warm. (oven)

It's in the pocket of something you wear when it's cold outside. (coat)

It's behind the thing you watch to see your favorite show. (television)

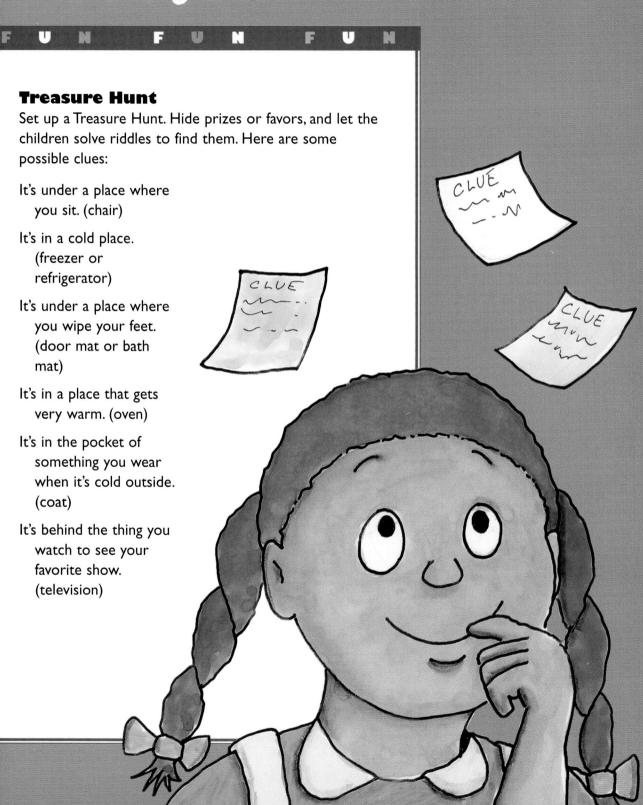

More Fun

Riddles

Here are a few you might try. For more, visit your library and look up some riddle books.

What letter of the alphabet is the coldest?

Iced "T"

Why are flowers so messy?

Because they never make their "beds"

What kind of song feels hard but is really good to eat?

A "rock 'n' roll" song

What's in Here?

Make a "feely box" by cutting a $2^1/_2$" hole in one end of a shoe box. Then cut the foot off of an old sock, leaving only the tube part. Tape or glue one end of the tube around the inside of the hole in the box; let the other end hang outside the box. Place several small objects inside the box, and put the lid on it. One at a time, let the children stick a hand through the sock into the box and guess which object they are touching.

Who Am I?

Cut several pieces of posterboard in half. Glue a picture of a different animal (cut from a magazine or coloring book) on each piece. Cut a small hole in each board for the children to look through. Have the children take turns standing behind a board without knowing which animal picture is on the other side. Let them look through the hole as they ask their friends yes-or-no questions about the pictured animal, until they can guess what the animal is.

Food

Mystery Snacks

Mystery Snacks

Put several kinds of candies or snacks in a paper bag. Use foods that children can recognize by touch, such as gummy worms, jelly beans, M&Ms®, and pretzels. Pass the sack around the circle of children. Have each child reach in without looking, grab a snack, and try to identify it before pulling it out and eating it.

Sherlock's Sherbet Punch

Mix your favorite sherbet (or sherbets) and ginger ale in a large punch bowl.

Sherlock's Sherbet Punch

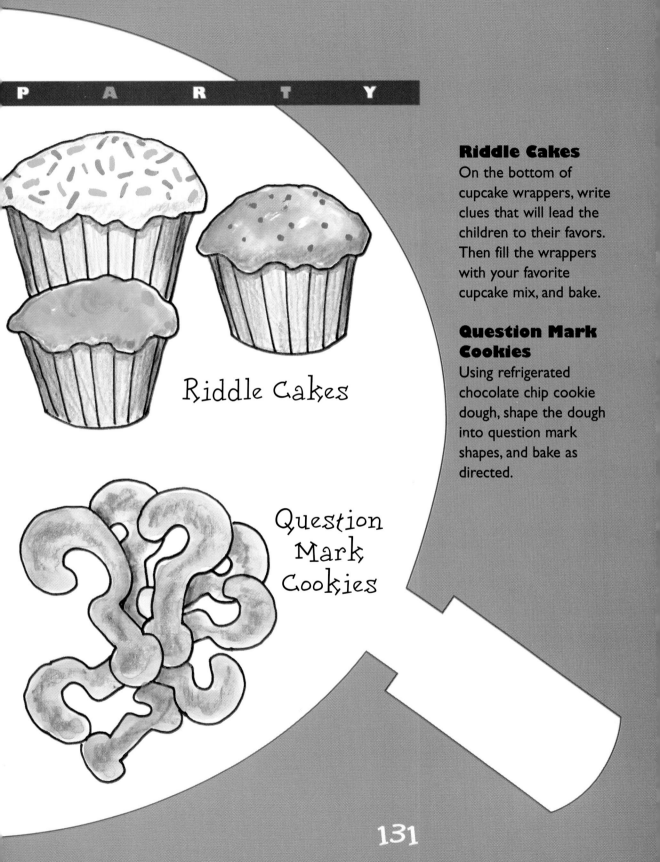

Riddle Cakes

Question Mark Cookies

Riddle Cakes

On the bottom of cupcake wrappers, write clues that will lead the children to their favors. Then fill the wrappers with your favorite cupcake mix, and bake.

Question Mark Cookies

Using refrigerated chocolate chip cookie dough, shape the dough into question mark shapes, and bake as directed.

Favors and Frills

Favors

Grab Bags

Prepare "grab bags" containing a few small objects, such as whistles, stickers, pencils, and so on. Let each child reach randomly into a cardboard box and take a grab bag home.

Hidden Picture

Photocopy the "hidden picture" sheet (see illustration) and give one to each child to take home.

Frills

Sherlock Holmes Costume

Wear a trench coat to the party. If you can find a Sherlock Holmes style hat, wear that too.

Decorate Walls

Decorate the walls with cutout footprints and question marks.

Fingerprints

Tape a piece of butcher paper on the wall near where children come in. Have them dip the tips of their fingers into a mixture of tempera paint and put their "fingerprints" on the paper.

Footprints

Place cutout footprints on the floor to direct traffic (see the pattern on page 133).

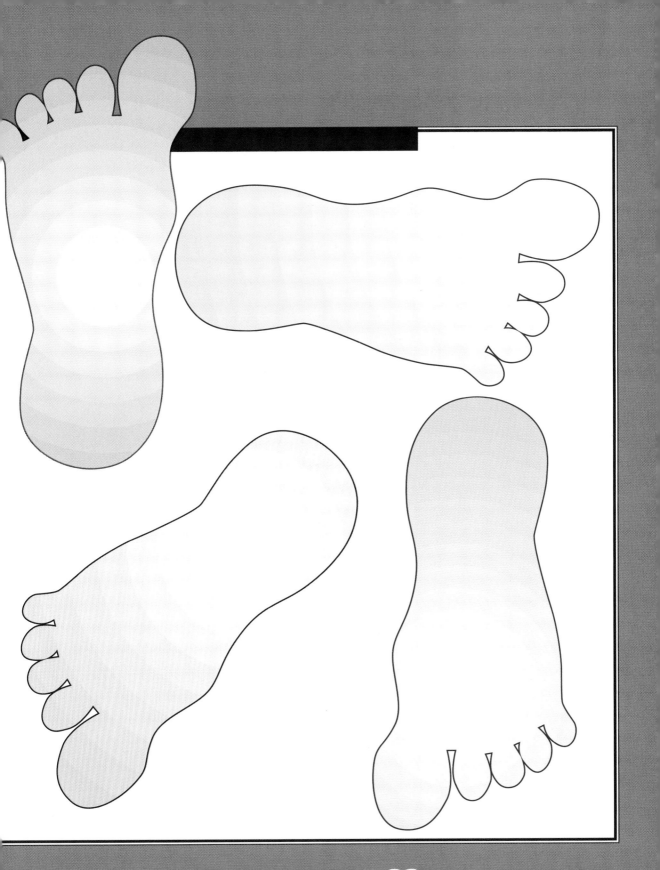

Facts

Some fictional detectives (such as Sherlock Holmes, Inspector Gadget, Nancy Drew, Encyclopedia Brown, and Cam Jansen) are very well known.

Sometimes detectives are called "gumshoes." The name comes from rubber- or gum-soled shoes that make very little noise; the wearer can sneak around quietly.

A mystery is a kind of puzzle. The clues to solve a mystery are like puzzle pieces.

Fiction

Allen, Pamela. *Who Sank the Boat?* Coward-McCann, 1983. A group of animal friends set off for a trip in a rowboat that is too small for them.

Eastman, P. D. *Are You My Mother?* Random House, 1960. A baby bird hatches from his egg while his mother is out, and he goes to find her.

Gardner, Beau. *Guess What?* Lothrop, 1985. The reader must identify animals by looking at only part of each one.

Hoban, Tana. *Look Again!* Macmillan, 1971. This collection of photographs shows part/whole relationships.

Munsch, Robert. *David's Father.* Annick, 1983. David's father is a very unusual person. But if you think he is strange, wait until you meet David's grandmother.

Tafuri, Nancy. *Have You Seen My Duckling?* Greenwillow, 1984. A mother duck searches for her duckling, who is mischievously hiding on each page.

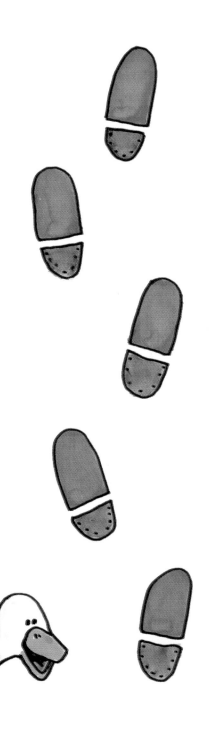

Parent/Child

Photocopy the front and back of the invitation and color both. Cut out both pieces and glue them back-to-back. For a sturdier invitation, "sandwich" a piece of construction paper between the two cutouts and glue all three pieces together. Your local "quick print" shop will probably have heavier weight sheets of colored paper onto which you can photocopy the front and back if you want to eliminate the coloring step. Place invitations into envelopes and mail to each guest.

You're Invited to a
Parent/Child Party

Party

This party is
being given by

....

Date: ....

Time: ....

Where: ....

....

....

Phone: ....

Fan-Fare

or

how to

invite

everybody

to the

party!

Parent/Child Party

Together Sculptures

Provide pipe cleaners, empty toilet paper tubes, empty boxes (from packages of oatmeal, potato chips, cereals, cookies, crackers, etc.), tissue paper, tempera paints, and glue. Let each parent and child pair create a sculpture and give it a name.

Three-Legged Race

Give each parent and child team a 2' length of rope to tie their ankles together. Prepare a start and finish line and let the teams race.

Straw Towers

Provide each parent and child pair with straws, tape, and scissors. See which team can build the highest tower using only the materials provided.

Hide and Seek

Let parents hide and children seek. Then reverse roles and play again.

Storytelling Circle

Ask each parent and child to tell the group a story about the funniest thing that's ever happened to them.

Food

Shoe Box Lunches

Pack a shoe box lunch for each parent and child pair. Put in two sandwiches, two apples, and two bags of chips. Let each parent and child find a place to sit together and share their lunch "picnic" style. You may want to lay three or four tablecloths on the floor or in the yard. Be sure to have an ice chest filled with sodas.

Shoe Box Lunches

Favors and Frills

P A R T Y

Photos

Take Polaroid® photos of each parent and child pair with their sculptures.

Favors

Frames

Make paper frames to fit the Polaroid® pictures. As the parent and child pairs arrive, take pictures of them. Tape the pictures in the frames for decorations.

Hands

Decorate the walls with big and little cutout hands. You could also hang them from the ceiling.

Frills

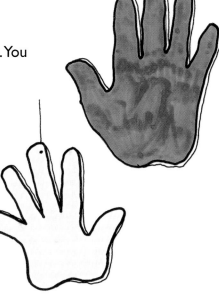

Facts

Parents who love their children

do their best to take care of them.

There are many variations of parent/child

relationships, including natural parents,

foster parents, adoptive parents,

and stepparents.

Fiction

Joose, Barbara M. *Mama, Do You Love Me?* Chronicle, 1991. A little girl tests the limits of her mother's love.

Ketteman, Helen. *Not Yet, Yvette!* Albert Whitman, 1992. A little girl has trouble waiting to present her mother's birthday surprise.

McCloskey, Robert. *Blueberries for Sal.* Viking, 1948. A little girl and a bear cub cross each other's path while out picking berries with their mothers.

Williams, Vera B. *A Chair for My Mother.* Mulberry, 1982. Rosa, her mother, and her grandmother save their money to buy a "wonderful, beautiful, fat, soft armchair."

Yolen, Jane. *Owl Moon.* Putnam, 1987. A father and young child go out on a moonlit night in search of an owl.

About the Authors

Dr. Pam Schiller has been a child-care center administrator, an assistant professor at the University of Houston, Clear Lake, a public school pre-K and kindergarten supervisor, vice president of Early Childhood and Staff Development for a major educational publisher, and president of the Southern Early Childhood Association. She has authored or co-authored many articles for early childhood journals as well as teacher resource books and has authored a complete curriculum for children ages three to six. Pam is the mother of two grown daughters and is the owner of Sydney, her pet iguana.

Mike Artell has written and/or illustrated dozens of picture books and teacher resource books and has hosted his own Saturday morning television cartooning show. Two of Mike's books have been chosen by *American Bookseller* magazine as "Pick of the Lists." Each year, Mike travels around the country helping teachers and students learn to think, write, and draw more creatively. Mike lives in Mandeville, Louisiana, with his wife and two daughters. Mike is a former class clown.